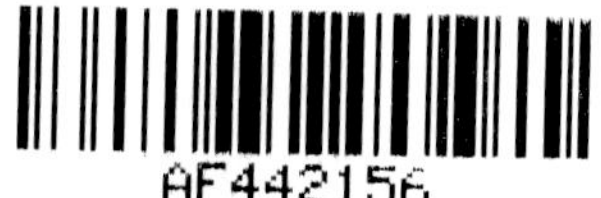

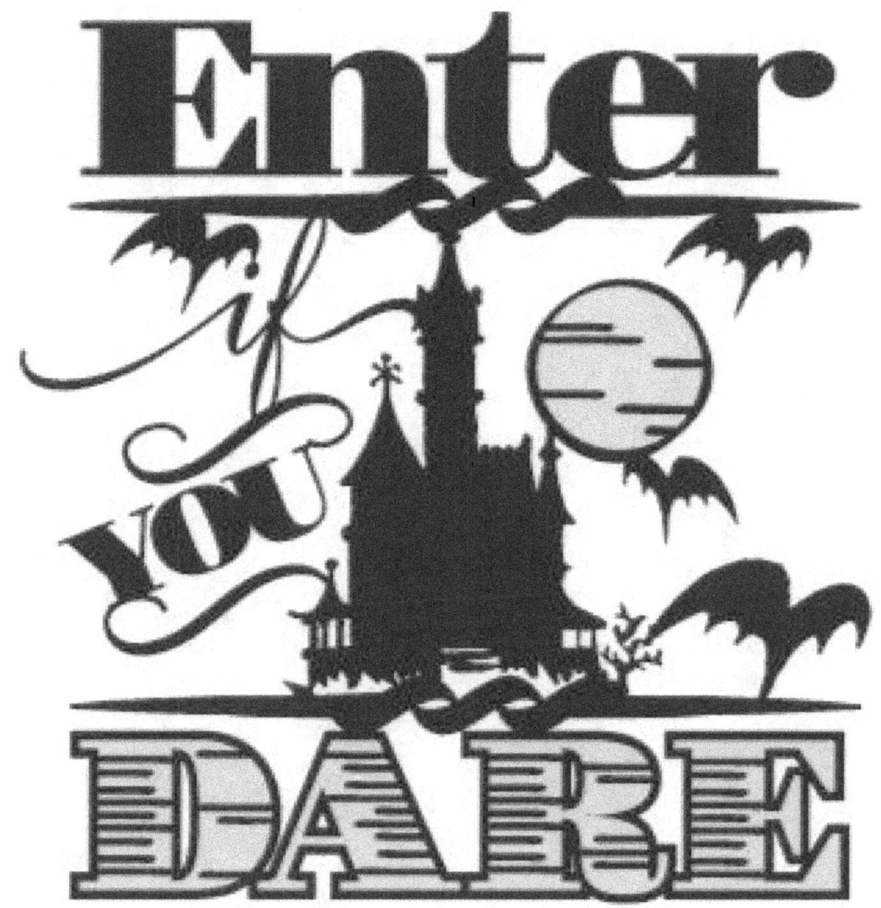

THIS BOOK BELONGS TO:

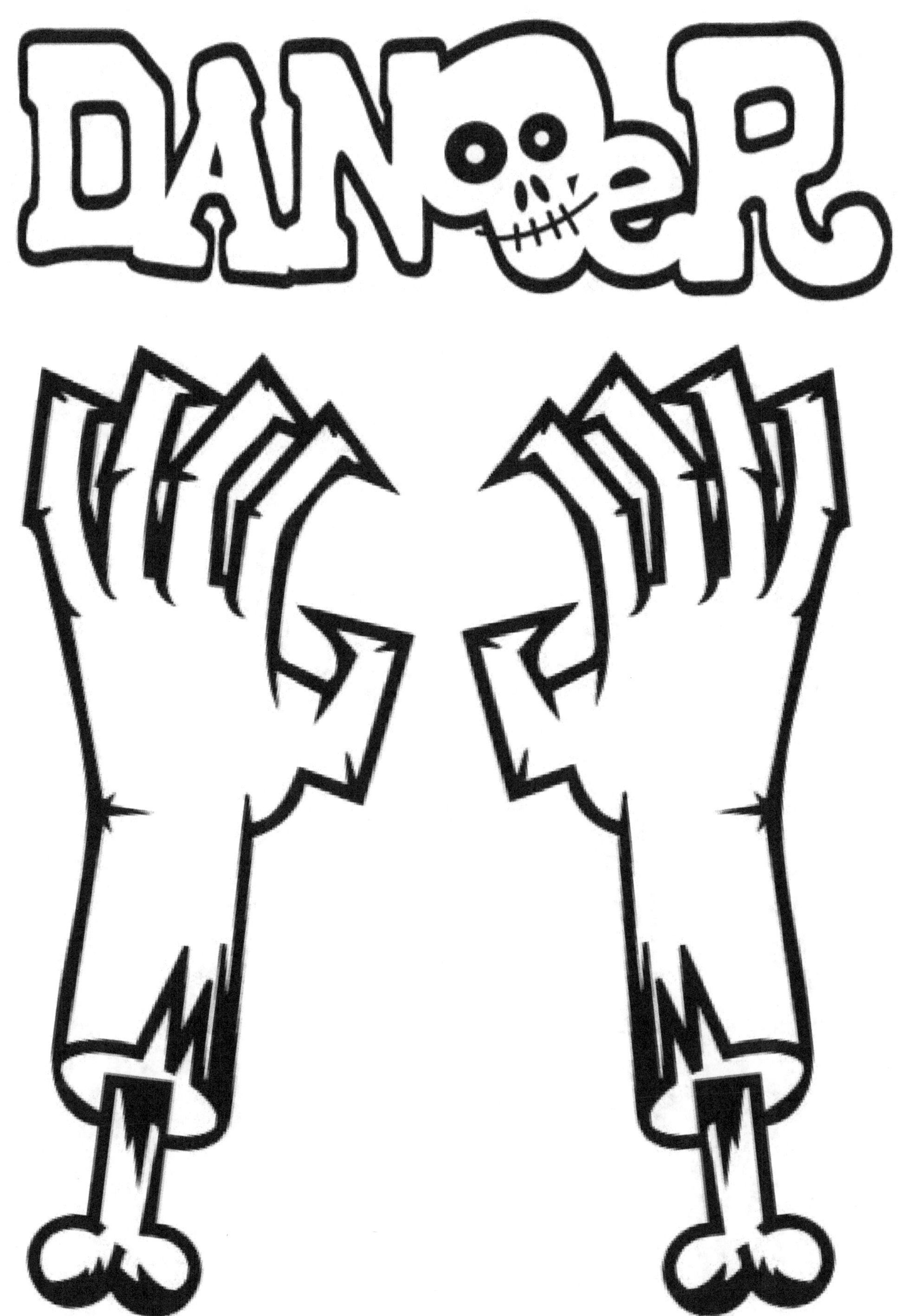
DANGER

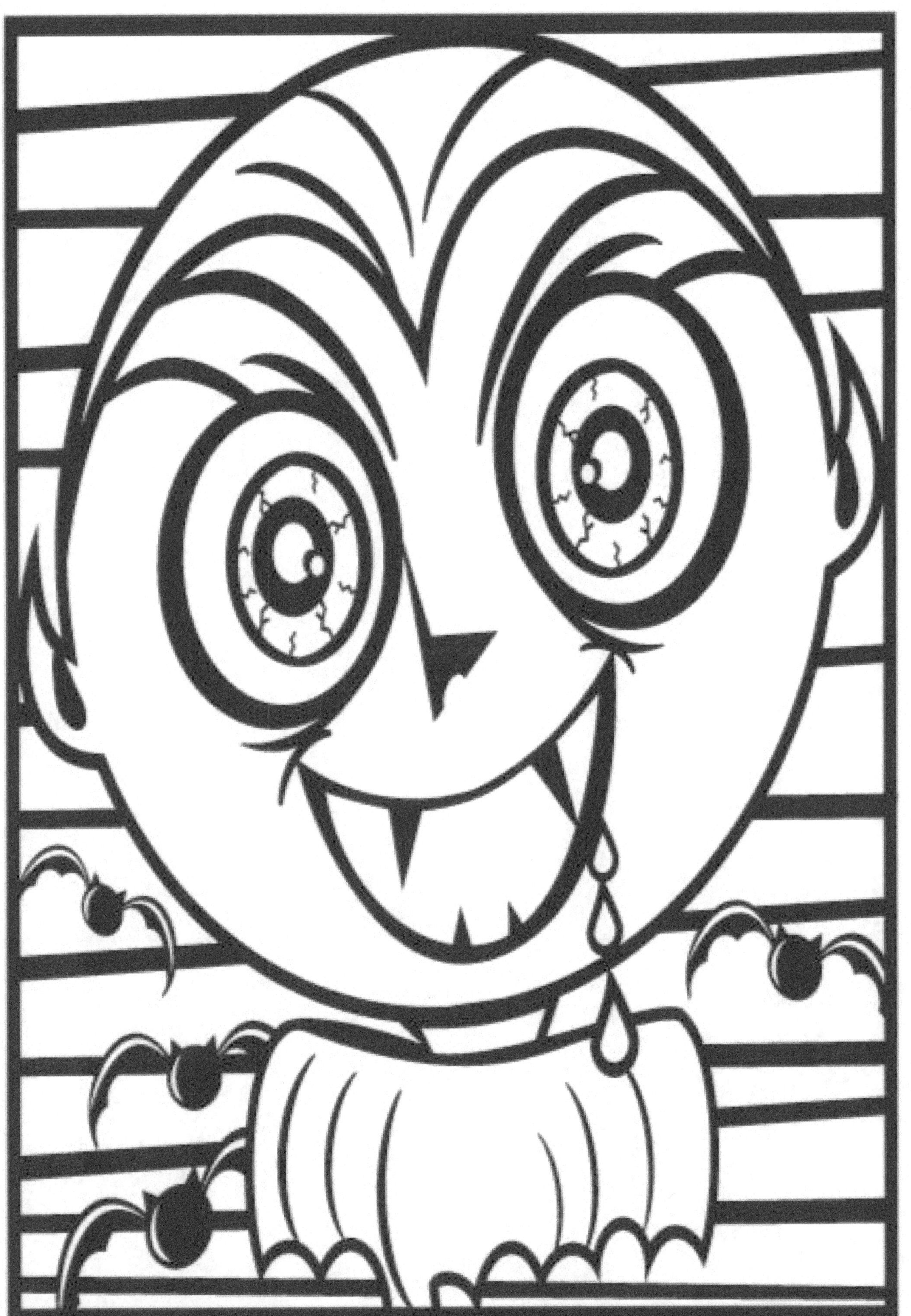

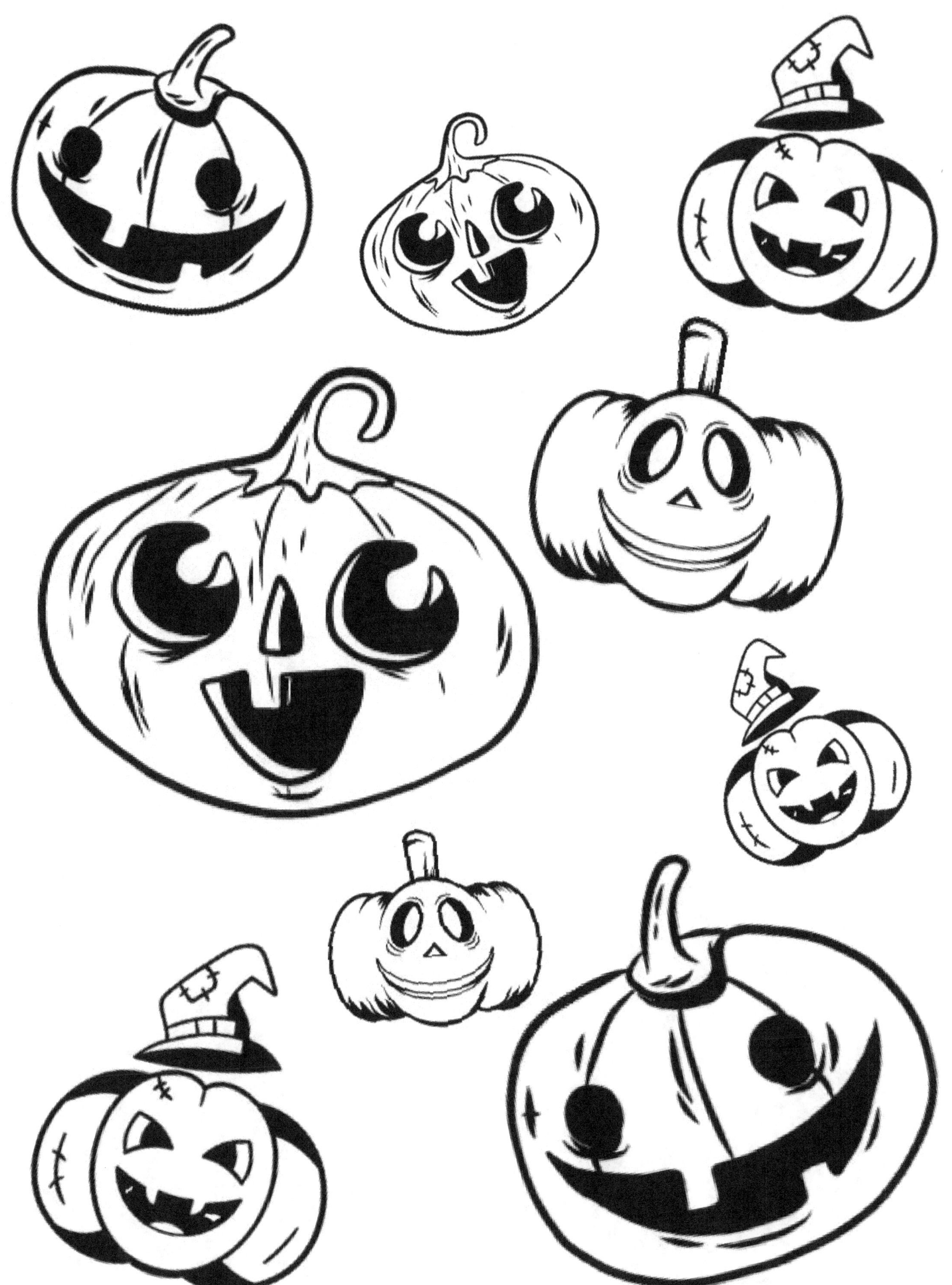

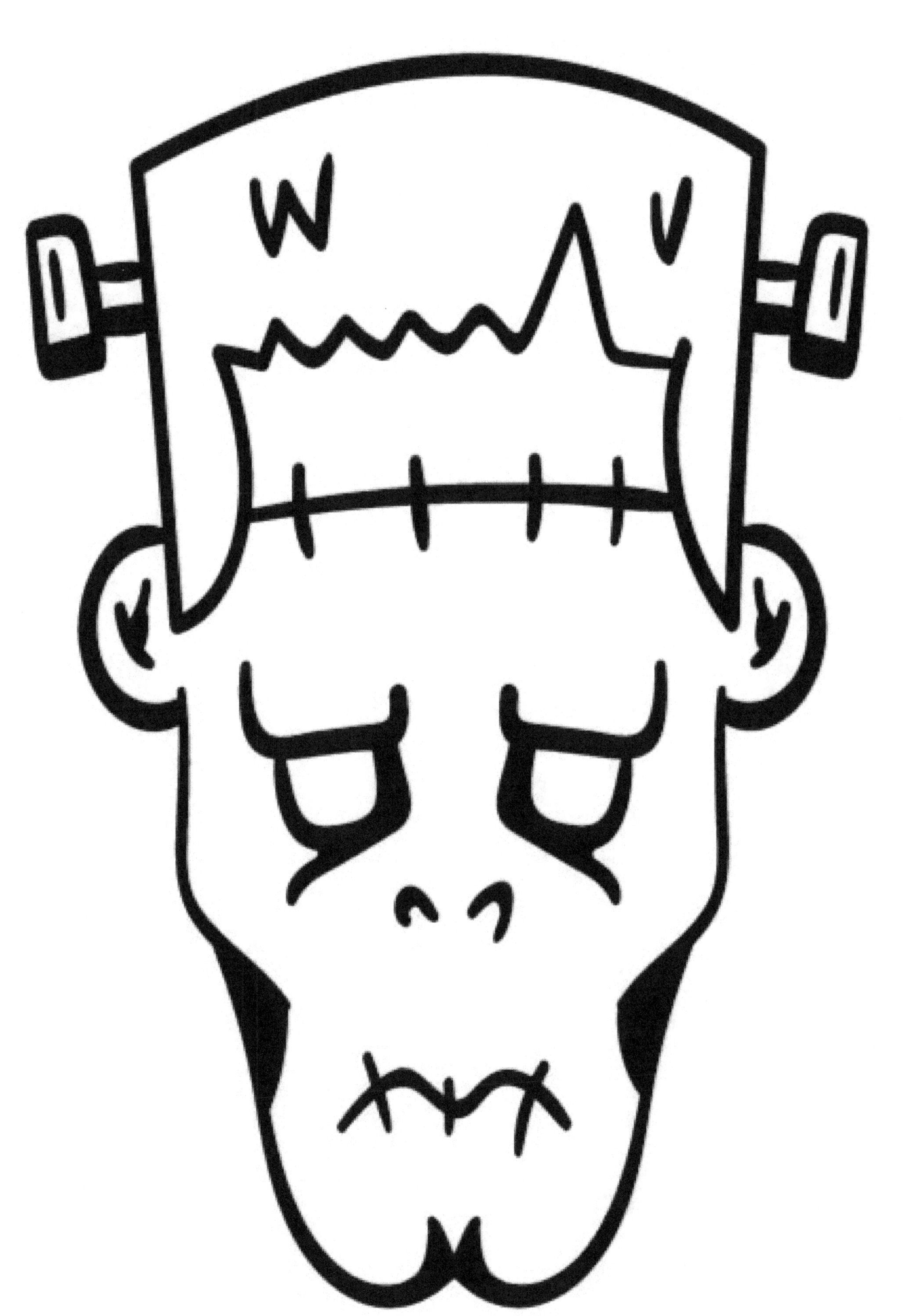

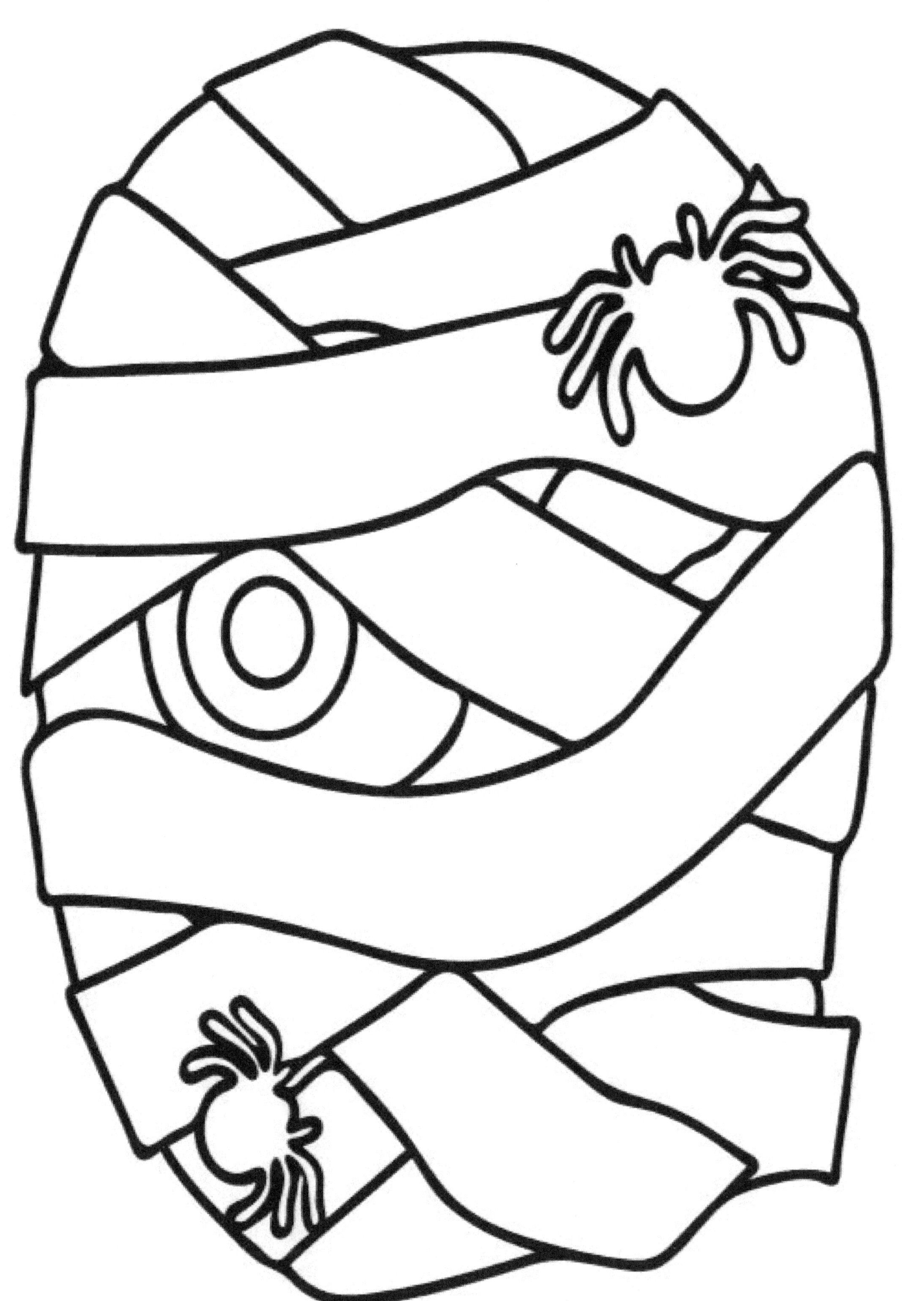

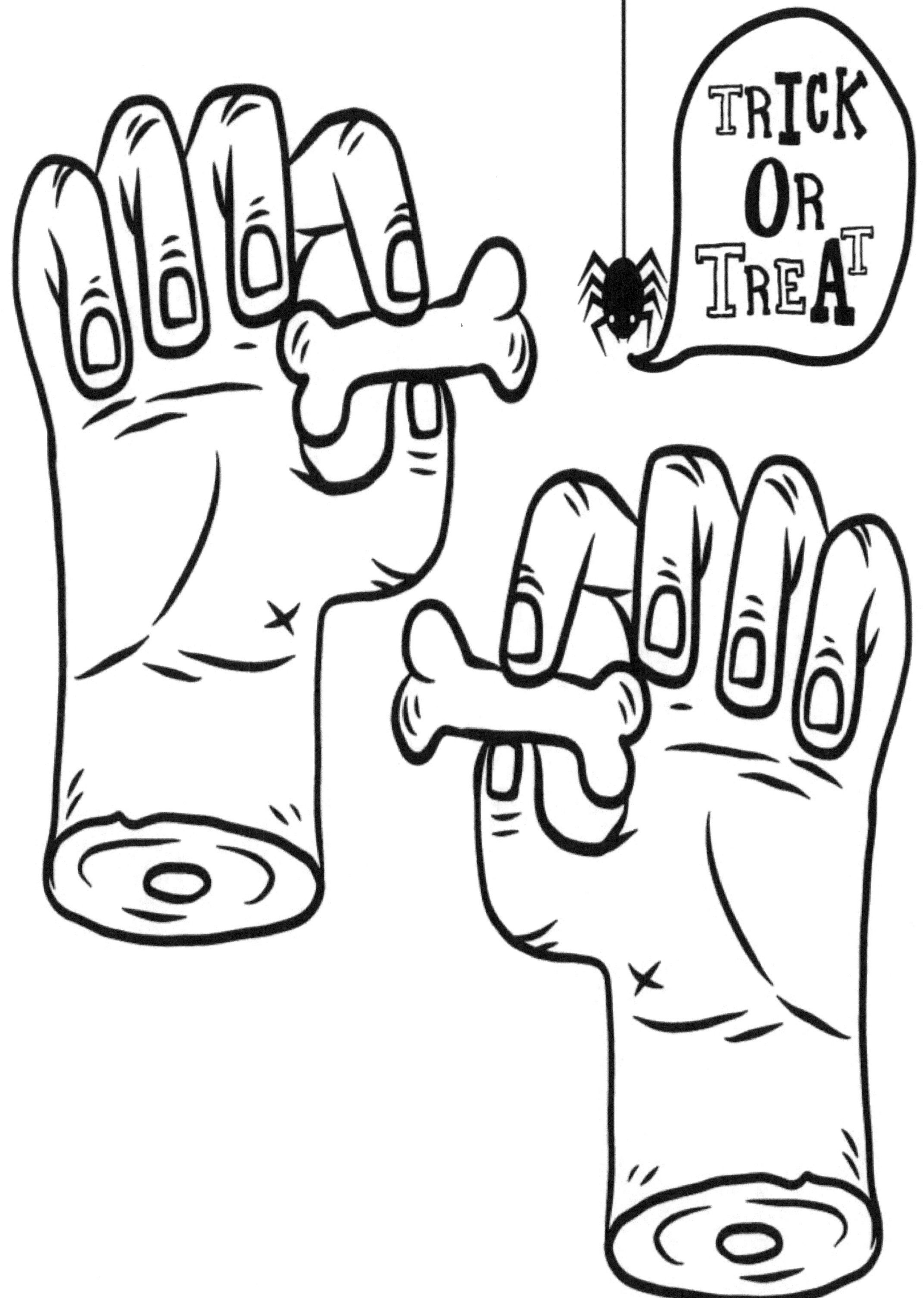

TRICK
OR
TREAT

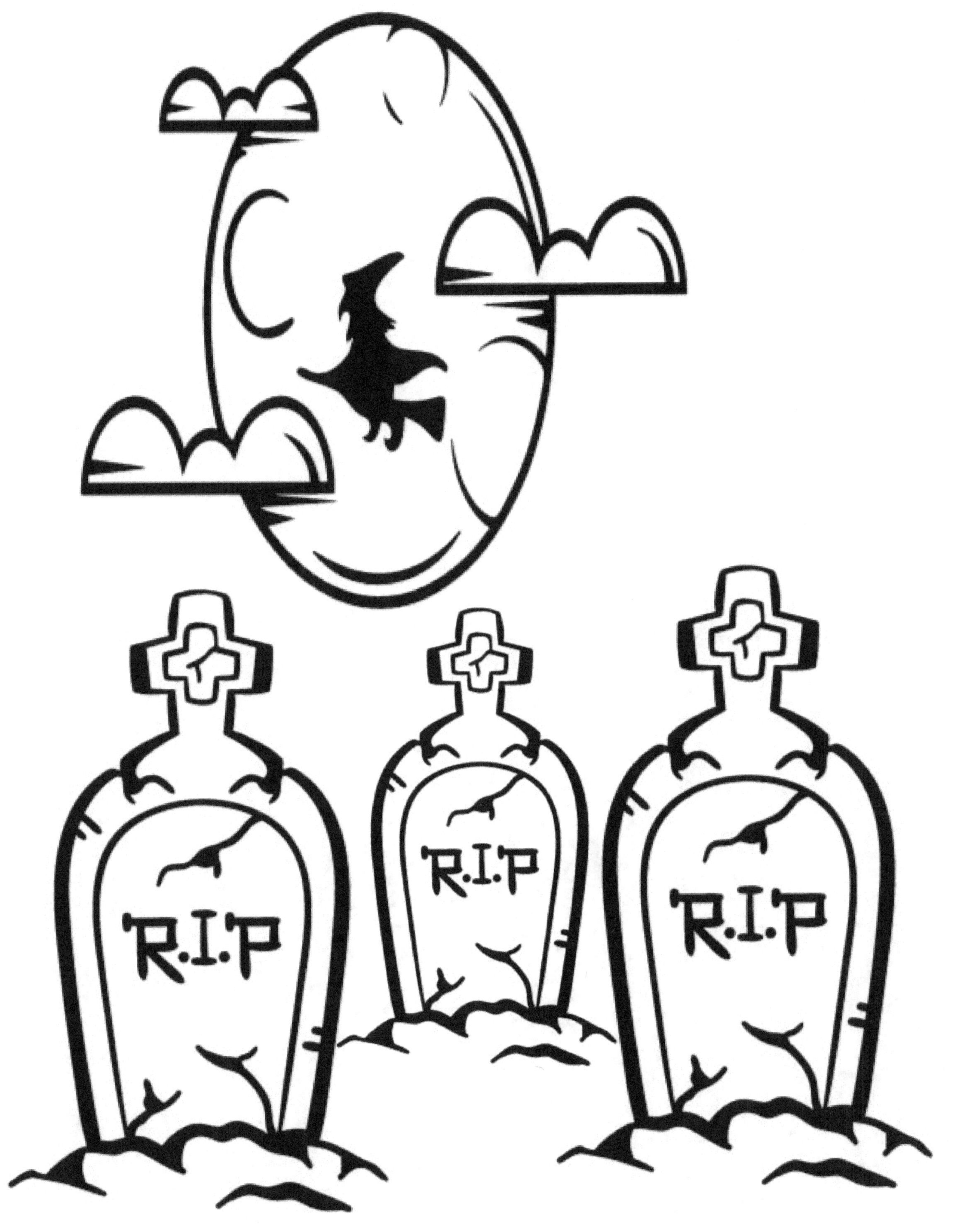

R.I.P
R.I.P
R.I.P

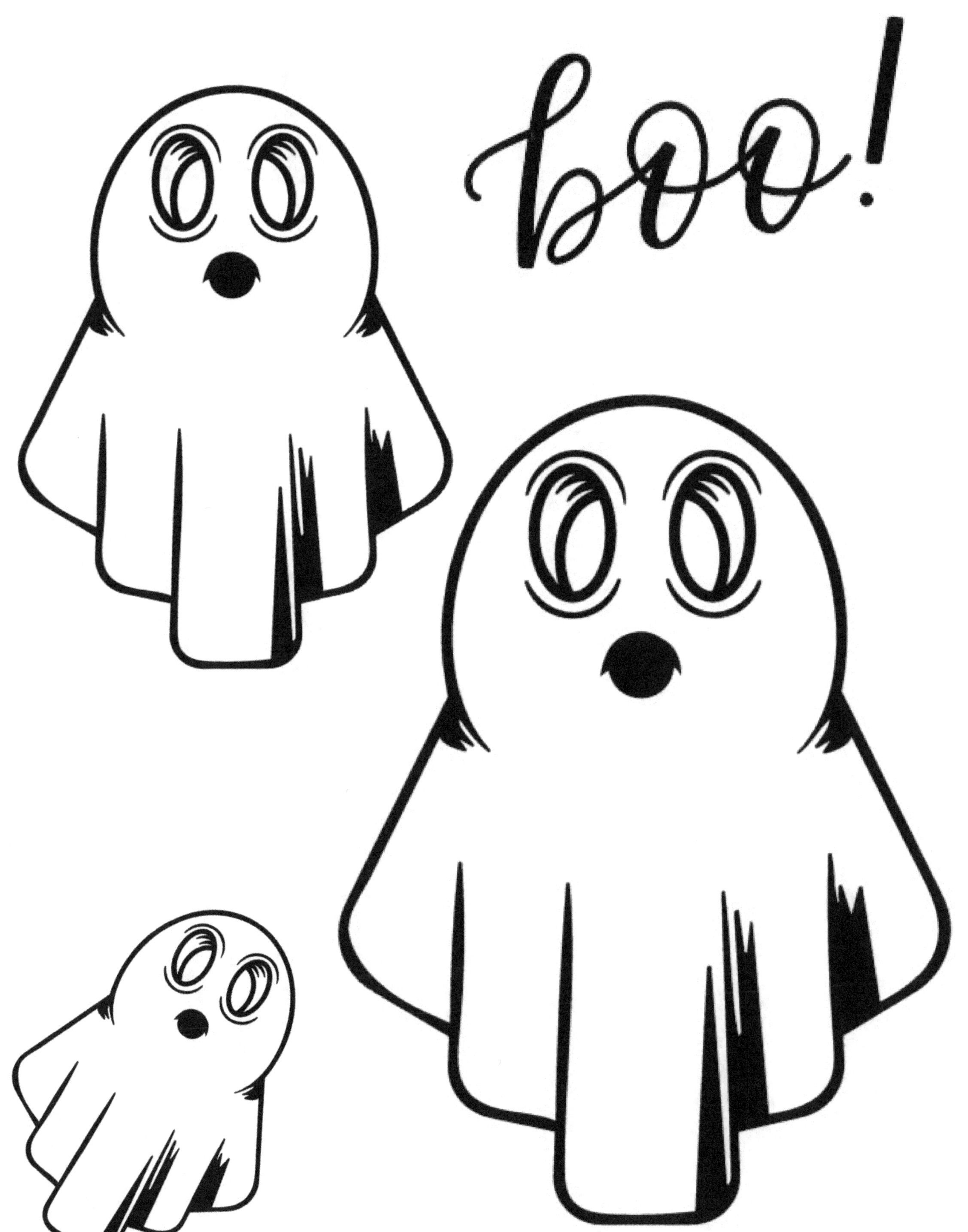

boo!

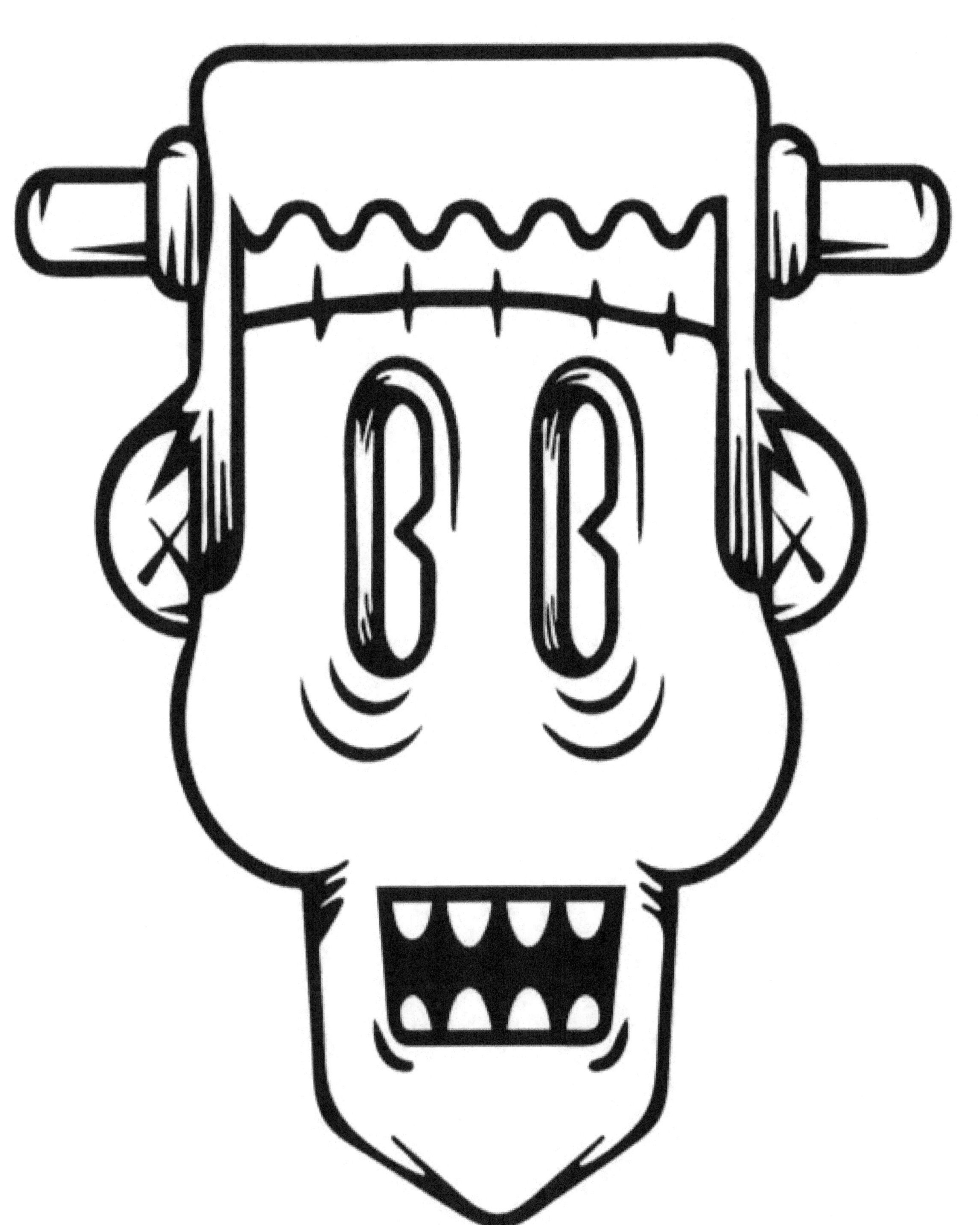

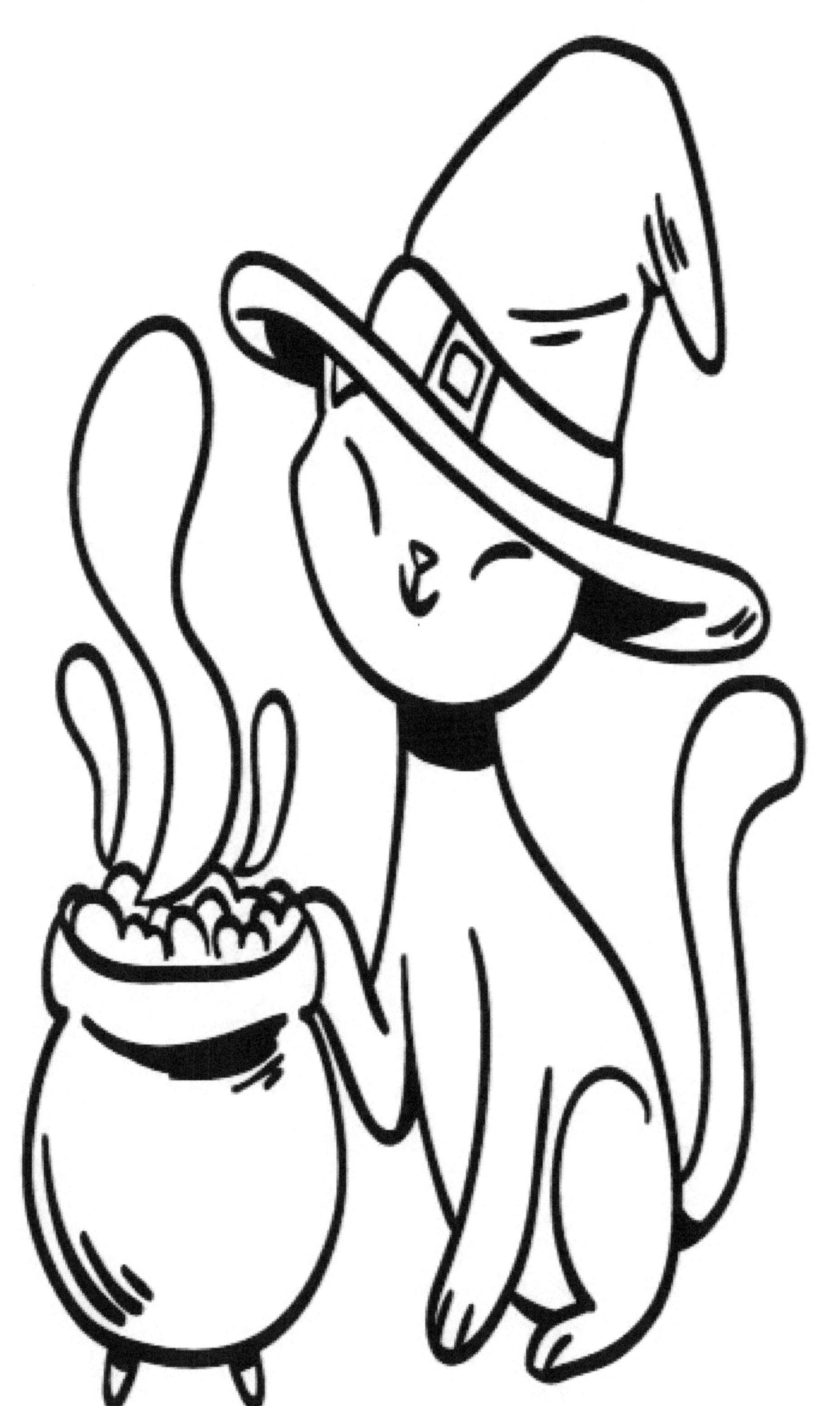

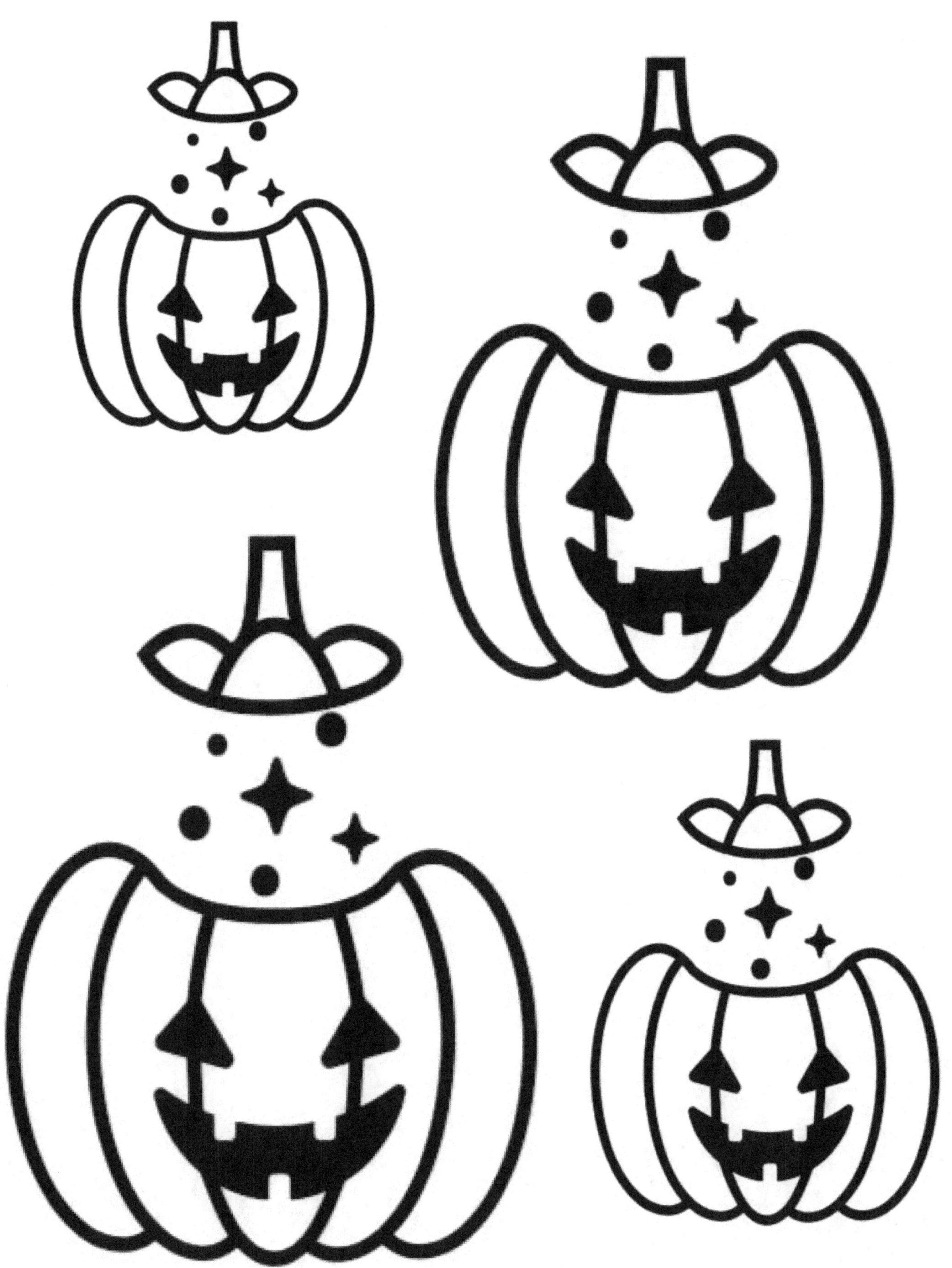

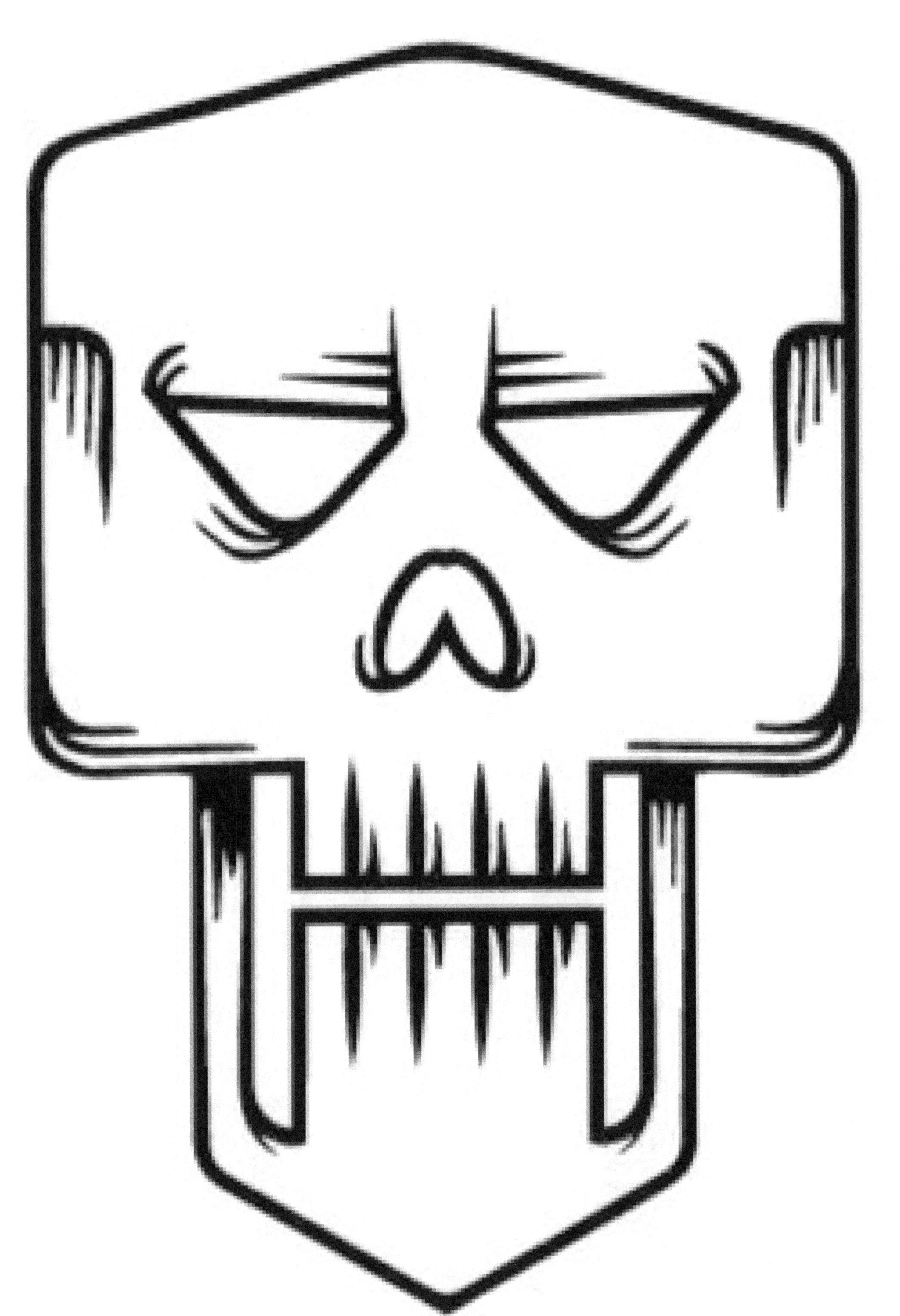

WITCHES
BREW

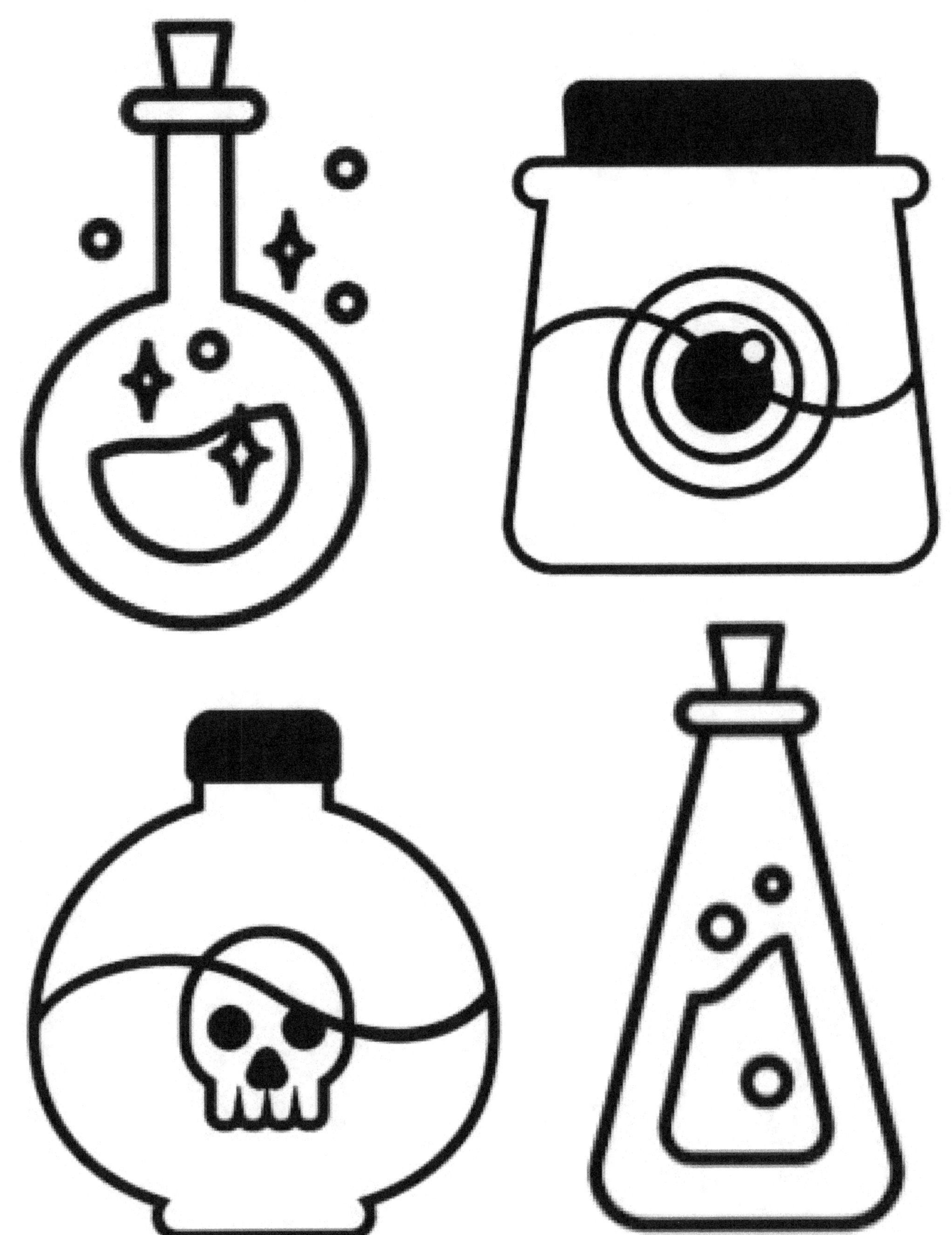

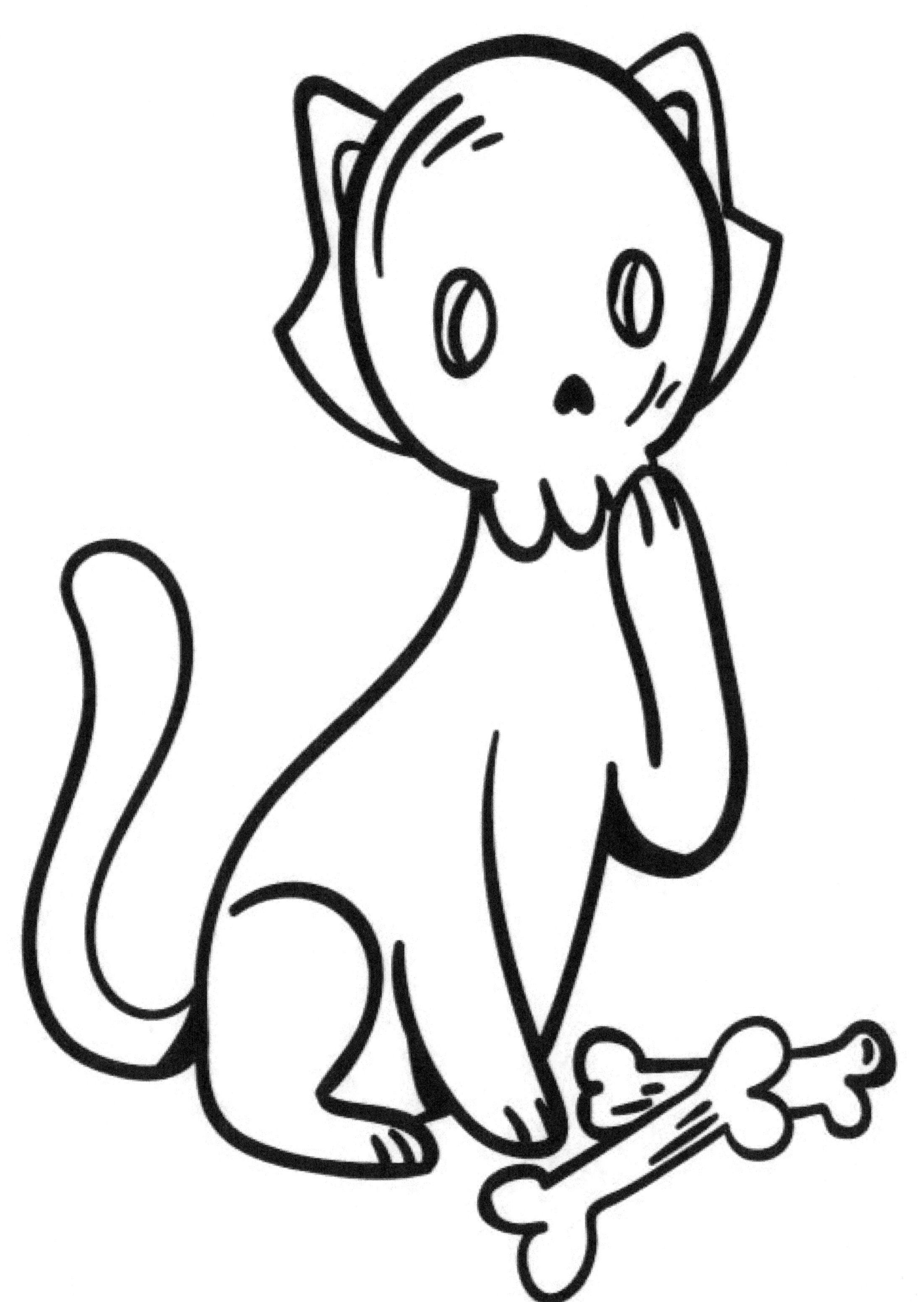

ZOMBIE

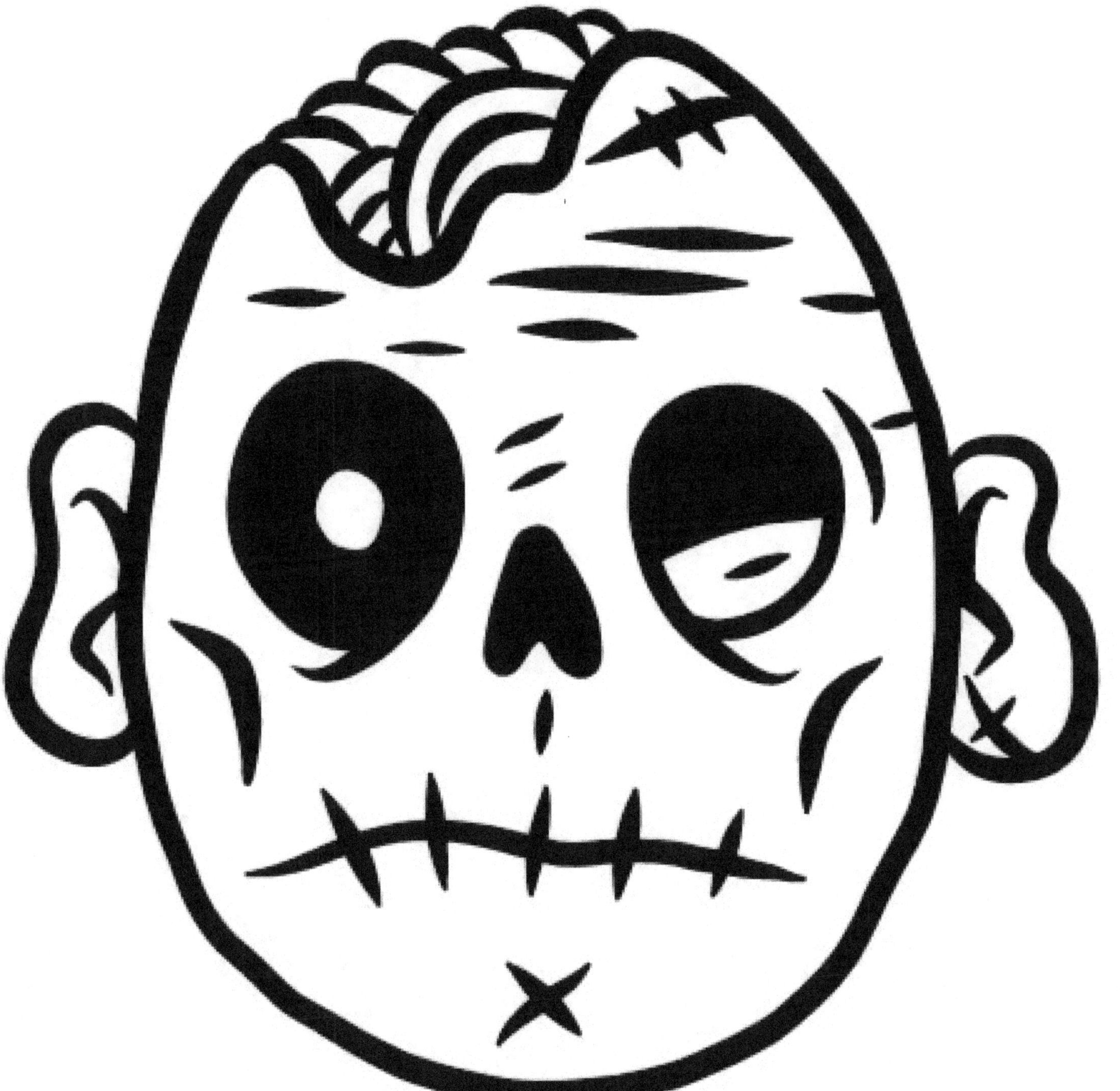

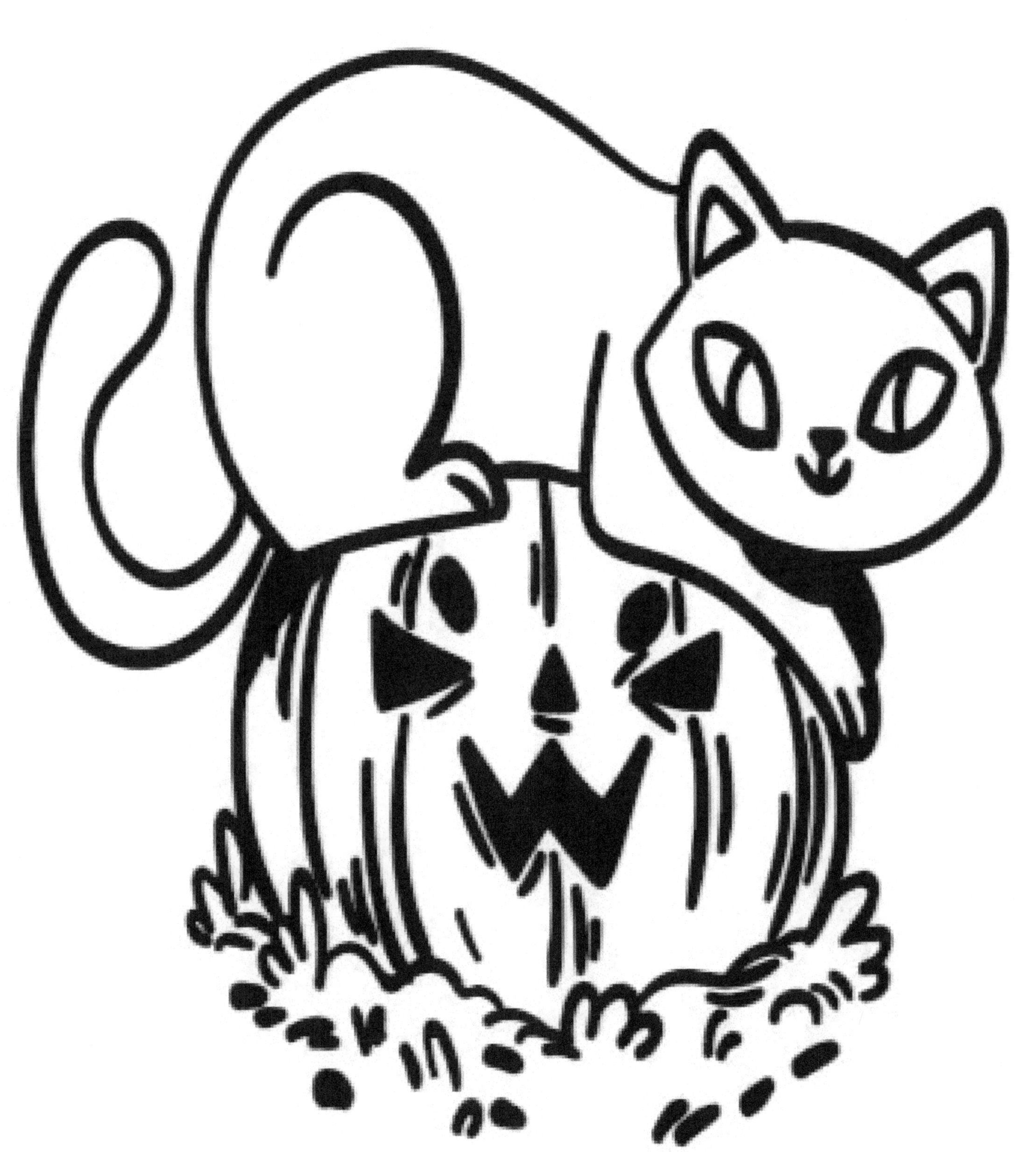

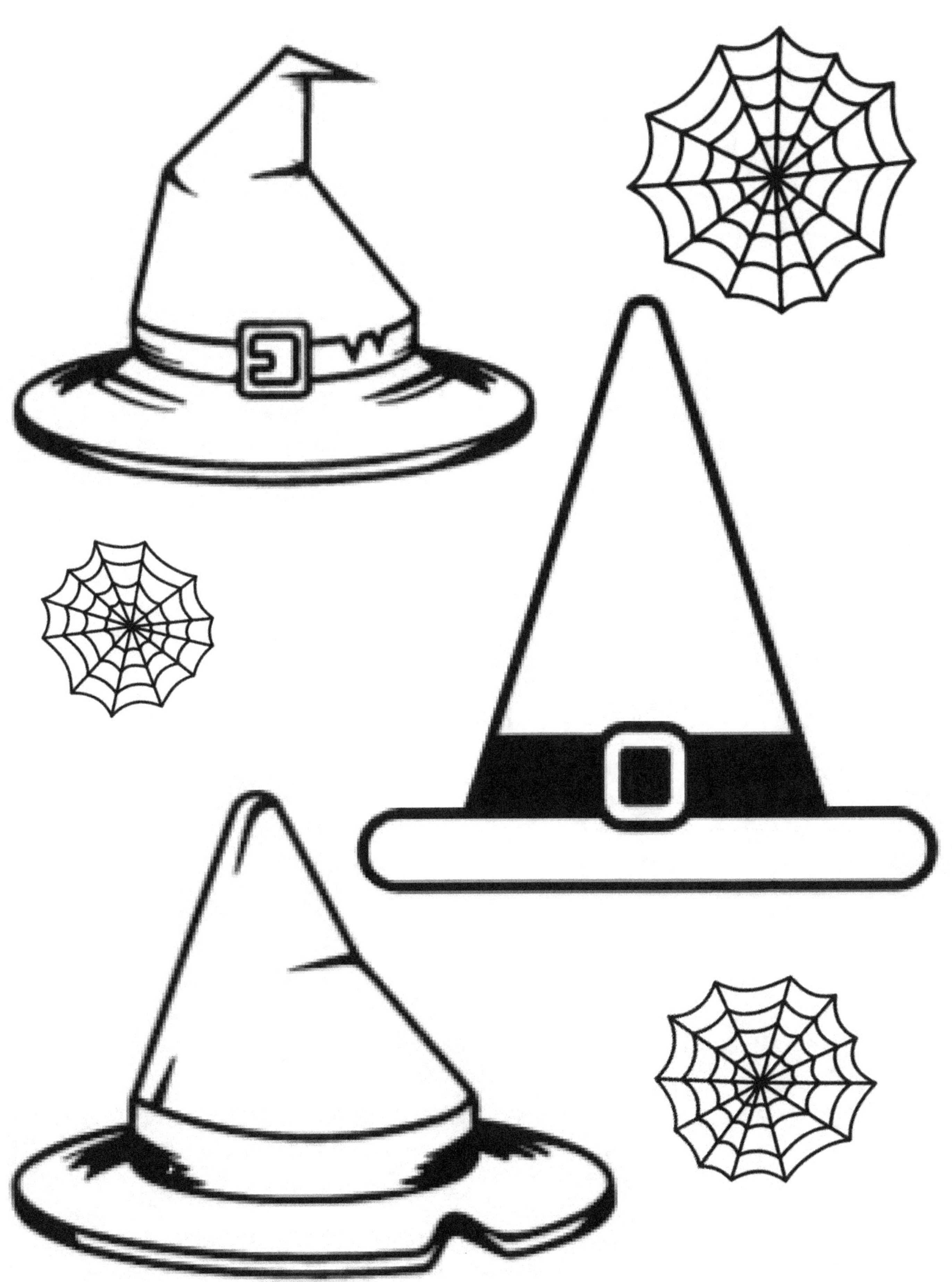

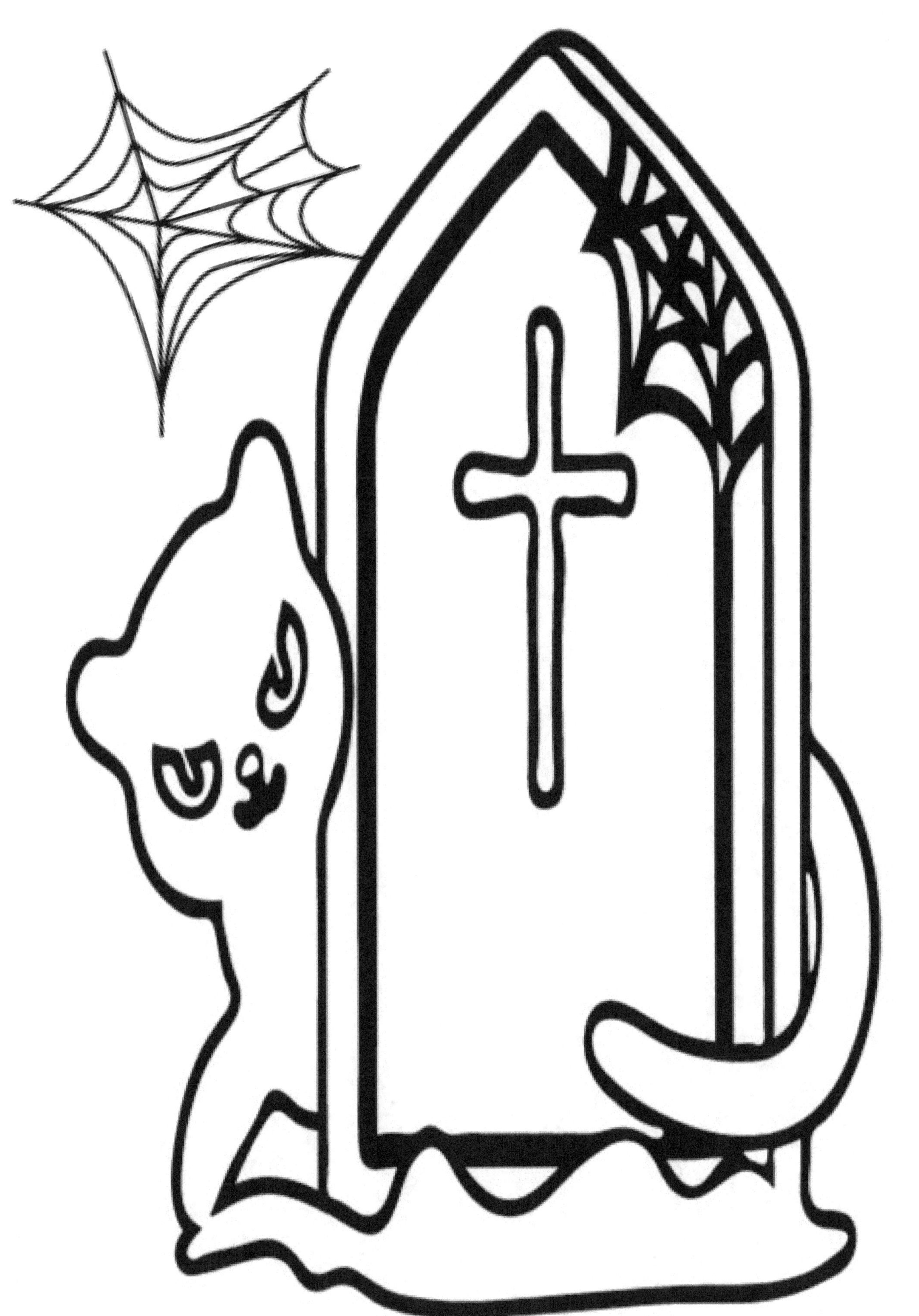